SPECIAL POWERS AND ABILITIES

Special Powers and Abilities

POEMS

Raymond McDaniel

COFFEE HOUSE PRESS
Minneapolis
2013

FOR ERIKA : I REALLY DON'T UNDERSTAND
QUITE WHY I AM SIGNING THIS BOOK
TO YOU RATHER THAN THE REVERSE —
AT WHICH TIME YOU WOULD THEN DROP
THE BOOK AND SHOUT BOOM, MR.
TOUGHIE! YOU! ARE! WELCOME!
BECAUSE, SEE, I AM SO GRATEFUL TO YOU
AND FOR YOU. I KNOW I AM UM
DIFFICULT. WITH GREAT LOVE &
HOPING FOR MORE CONVERSATION IN THE
FUTURE. EARLIER THAN 30th CENTURY!

Coffee House Press books are available to the trade through our primary distributor, Consortium Book Sales & Distribution, cbsd.com or (800) 283-3572. For personal orders, catalogs, or other information, write to: info@coffeehousepress.org.

Coffee House Press is a nonprofit literary publishing house. Support from private foundations, corporate giving programs, government programs, and generous individuals helps make the publication of our books possible. We gratefully acknowledge their support in detail in the back of this book. To you and our many readers around the world, we send our thanks for your continuing support.

Good books are brewing at coffeehousepress.org

LIBRARY OF CONGRESS CATALOGING-IN-PUBLICATION DATA
McDaniel, Raymond, 1969–
Special powers and abilities / by Raymond McDaniel. — 1st ed.
p. cm.
ISBN 978-1-56689-315-2 (alk. paper)
1. Title.
PS3613.C3868S64 2013
813´.6—DC23
2011046607

Printed in the United States
1 3 5 7 9 8 6 4 2
FIRST EDITION | FIRST PRINTING

The poems in this volume ponder, satirize, valorize, melodramatize, manipulate, refer to, comment upon, and occasionally cite characters and plots associated with Adventure Comics, Superboy and the Legion of Super-Heroes, and the Legion of Super-Heroes, all published by DC Comics, a subsidiary of Warner Bros. Rights to characters is neither claimed nor implied, and the poems are not intended to supplant, replace, or be mistaken for the associated comic book properties. The author thanks the very, very many editors, writers, artists, inkers, colorists, letterers, and fans who have contributed to the rich legacy of the Legion of Super-Heroes.

SPECIAL POWERS AND ABILITIES

Gold

Silver

Bronze

Welcome, Visitors

Is this your first visit to the 30th century?

Those of you from a millennium past may experience disorientation.

Know that we have addressed our epoch to utopia.

Know that we looked to you when we designed the answer to the question of our future, a fiction.

See this flag, this florid banner, this gaiety and riot.

See this golden tower, which resembles an inverted rocket ship.

Look up, and see the sky teem with the teens of ten thousand suns.

A legion.

What to Expect

Sibling rivalry persists.

Girls have come to trust girls but boys will be boys, dumb, stupidly sentimental.

Dim, almost-divine boys still race ahead, even after you ask them not to. Paragods with their girls in their arms go *whoosh* and *zoom*.

We lose our minds more often than we might like.

There will be hair pulling, but as a rule we still stand on ceremony.

We are shopping for our girlfriends when we are challenged to duels, to tests, to expressions of worthiness.

Androids are a problem. They always will be.

Someone is always pulling off a mask and saying *surprise!*

Some still murder, just for the thrill of it.

Telepathic pets prove sentient.

Adults resent us, owe us, insist upon us.

We still get sick: Rigel fever, VSR virus, pain plague, heartache, nostalgia.

Lots of impostors, mirror images, inversions, and betrayals.

We don't need more than the identities we already have.

Sometimes we are tracking a fierce astrovulture. Sometimes, a galactosaur.

Somehow there is money without poverty and somehow without poverty people still want to steal.

World War VI was fought in 2783 with superweapons wielded by computer minds but all that is so, so long ago.

We fall for games, fads, and outrageous fashions.

We get killed, of course, but don't always die.

Crystals, in their approximation of life, replace memorial flowers, which are left to live and die without our interruption.

Our adolescent vanity is justifiable.

We will grow up. But we will never grow old.

Gold

The galaxy is suffused with radio noise even without the billions of citizens of the United Planets and their chatter and babble, so think of us as corporeal occupants of the broadcast superband, the wavelength on which messages preempt whatever's raucous to prevent future chaos. We aren't government, at least not in the way the governors sit, superficies, on the ground of the governed. We are just here to help. We are supercharged with a task. Yes, it is everyone's task, but ours especially. Consider us super-induced, added to that which is, enumerated perhaps to the point of being supererogative if never quite superfluous, each one of us supernumerary, all of us superhetrodyne, mixed, reactive, multiple, magical. At our best we are a superorganism, a whole of many parts, at our worst a superstructure, a scaffold that barely holds together. At our best we approach superfluidity, frictionless in action if never so at rest.

In confidence,
Brainiac 5

Saturn Girl / Imra Ardeen of Titan / Telepathy

ever constant, she sounds like conscience	distant and distaff
her mind reels and spins	affected telepath
icy moon and icy moods	*oh don't mind me*
her thoughts know no boundary	secret-keeper but poison to privacy
speechless, for what's the need	she declares herself in our ideas
unmediated, mental	something just occurred to her
she gets in your head	you are always in her thoughts

Lightning Lad / Garth Ranzz of Winath / Lightning

hot-headed red-headed finger-snapper	charged, then changed
struck twice, unlucky lad	you jump up to get beat down
battered battery	sometimes limbless, sometimes dead
but always fecklessly electrical	the wire alive
he casts hot & fast	breaching branches
your herald's charge	energetic ahead
spark & spar	blunt thunderer

Cosmic Boy / Rokk Krin of Braal / Magnetism

come together	the first is a fundamental force
mediator, lodestone, & needle	magnetoceptor
brooding boy	like a big brother
megamannered and conscientious	he brings us closer
his temper keeps everything in check	our genius loci
a warper, a distorter	impeccably ordered
as is every leader	attractive in black

Saturn Girl Loves Lightning Lad

There's a reason why "matronizing" isn't a word
it concerns mothering
and who on Earth or Earth-like worlds would want such a thing.
Take Lightning Lad,
legendarily unlucky in everything except his choice of girlfriend,
but we can't call that luck
because she can receive and project thoughts and has no time
for foolishness
except when it comes to him. If anyone's made a choice here
it's her,
because she could do better—maybe even best—
as in Cosmic Boy,
her best friend and Lightning Lad's, too. They seem the better pair:
both sane, both stable,
and that's why they don't stand a chance; she's too good
to leave LL at a loss
and so is Cosmic Boy, which means that in the end
Garth loves Imra
because she is the intersection of best friend and ingénue
which leaves Rokk
to love them less together than each separately. They say
a triangle
is the most stable structure, but actually that's a pyramid,
three sides
but with four points, one of which is the apex, the highest,
sharpest point,

the corner that affords the greatest view. A love triangle
would be easier,
but don't bother telling Saturn Girl, whose childhood sweetheart
will become
more child and less sweet as her mind replaces her heart.

Duo Damsel / Luornu Durgo of Cargg / Triplication powers

once a triplicate	previously primary
duplication endlessly rejects point of view	*"I said that"*
"no, I said that"	who becomes which
fewer than deserved	even diminished Duo agrees to regret
to embargo individual	another other
"what do you think?"	*"what do you think?"*
she declenses	she selves to defend

Phantom Girl / Tinya Wazzo of Bgztl / Intangibility

apparent apparition	most present when half past
bedecked in black & white	neither here nor there
stitched of silk & almost-oblivion	plain tart & sharp tongue
pert	positioned to touch without being touched
her whole planet's a sham	impossible to pin down
never quite	go-go ghostly
almost abstract	always coming or going

Superboy

Clark Kent of Earth	Kal-El of Krypton
gosh	artifact of the era of alter egos
glorious skyward	upward away
ordinary steady	best as boyish
role model	unbreakable mold
country-come-to-town	the blessed best of us
ignorant of sin and ignorant as	real strong goodness
our moral immortal	the teen of steel

Superboy Does Not Love Duo Damsel

I've come to you
just to see you do
what I know you'll do

which is leave her even though
it will look as if she is leaving you
and I know that and so does Claude Rains

and maybe Conrad Veidt
but not everyone here tonight
mixed-up crowd and a few crickets

and these girls I'm with
each monotwins
in the backseat of Pa's car

she's spooky, these two,
well she wanted to see some
gothic space movie

living intestines and dead intestines
but I wanted to see you
just like you wanted that same old song

even though it was no darn good—

I've spent all day in the future pool
chemical stink and age
for skin less than steel

these girls finish each other's sentences
'gosh I'd like' 'a root beer?'
I'm ganged up and outnumbered

when one of her slides
from the inflatable dolphin
and says she thinks I am keen

a weak solution
of Halloween payday & rust
but for just a second

I think it is the other
whose lips are moving
anyways, I know

every word to this movie
except what the Nazis say
and the boring bits in Paris

but yes to the airport scene
and all the banter and I'm asking you
how can you be so sure

about what you don't want?

Chameleon Boy / Reep Daggle of Durla / Shape changing

radical relativist

keeper of a fluid zoo

metaphorical metamorph

all shapes forthcoming

proof of both surface and substance

catholic in your tastes

unimpeachable approximator

polymorphous prankster

golden antennae tuned to comfort

he espies with his little eye

easily impressed upon

beastly and ubiquitous

and at home everywhere

sincerest polyform flatterer

Colossal Boy / Gim Allon of Earth / Supergrowth

essentially an officer of the law

wishful, wistful, bashful

more boy

he raises the roof

a good son makes a good target

substantive, massive, major

the fool who rushes in

hugely good-natured

what makes a good boy better?

embiggened

he has this well in hand

he takes up all the air in the room

reluctant to grow up

he falls hard

Invisible Kid / Lyle Norg of Earth / Invisibility

second-smartest

lab lad & lab rat

curious to perceive, to know

a hider with plain sight

a serum swallower

light bender, broken

devotee of an undetectable heaven

our sane salutatorian

first test for each of his own hypotheses

erasing gaze

auto-effacer

maker of potions & proposals

well-spoken

we'll never see you again

Nobody Loves Chameleon Boy

Who can't get a date,

tells himself *people are too superficial*,

conveniently ignores the imperative to define *superficial enough*,

knows that's funny coming from him,

is orange and bald,

is the first alien who looks, you know, alien,

wonders why anyone wouldn't want a shape changer,

thinks anyone superficial would think that was the greatest thing ever,

is too alien to know your date wants to know who you really are,

will never learn that no one actually wants to know that,

won't find out how ghastly any given "real you" really is,

will have his most meaningful relationship with a blob of protoplasm,

is whomever,

is skin-deep.

Star Boy / Thom Kallor of Xanthu / Inducement of mass

proverbial ton of bricks
with heavy heart
you make us groan
a buffoon
the weight of your devotion to her
a singularity
clumsy a quitter

look, you suck
"I don't think you see the *gravity* of the situation!"
your jokes float like lead balloons
Dream Girl's beard
collapsing on itself until hole
a sunken hope
you just fell into this gig

Brainiac 5 / Querl Dox of Colu / Superintelligence

bred for reason
smug in his elaboratory
special intelligence, digital will
he can never throw anything away
some quotient hysteric
force, his insurance
he who earned admission

his attention like ice & addition
his equations equal etiology
he needs no formulae
hopeless hypodermic
his wits about
authority, your aura
because untouchable

Supergirl / Kara Zor-El of Krypton

the dead world's last girl
she doesn't like you that way, ok?
too true to be human
funny, friendly
the day's savior, our gladiatrix
bears her burden brightly
but does right lightly

subjective perfection
best friend, blessed friend
plenipotentiary
well aren't *you* sweet
she shrugs it off
does right
she says she's the luckiest girl in this world

Brainiac 5 Models the Bottle City of Kandor

Terraria and transistors plucked from the dragonfly:
map of simple circuits, last city of Krypton, proud Kandor.

It is the work of my inculcation year, my majority.
Aching walls raised then razed, map made from memory.

Here, its fountain of fluid sentience, this thimble filled
with cold blue dye, almost-ice, its elegant intelligence.

I know time works differently for the very small. Superboy,
dumb but dazzling, miniature messiah by which the city's saved.

Conductive coil snug around a bartered battery's lip becomes
the memorial torch of Kandor, urban remainder, elapsed capital,

where all deeds are possible because its horizon knows no ring.
It is my progenitor, the Prime, who stole this bottled city,

bolted forth with her millions, their gardens and galleries
tucked snug under his arm. Stories always say Superboy

gave chase as only an orphan can. My instructors bemoan this apocrypha
as waste, drone against my incipient emotion for this fraction place.

But when I drown my Kandor—angry architect, five times—I aim
the pneumatics at the planet's last until the water shades down

the dome, enormous sheet. This will become my time, my shrink ray.
Its past my mastery, its path my presence, its god my girl.

I will become smaller than unregulated rain, I will fall between
drops, globes that adopt the size of whole and beautiful worlds.

Brainiac 5 Loves Supergirl

Brainiac 5 loves Supergirl

        Supergirl loves Brainiac 5

        Supergirl will love

Brainiac 5 once she meets   Brainiac 5

by the time   Supergirl meets Brainiac 5

        Supergirl will have been dead one thousand years

Brainiac 5 wants Supergirl to get to know him

        because Brainiac 5 will go back in time to meet

        Supergirl who will be alive one thousand years ago

        Supergirl will also be alive a thousand years from then

due to the lunatic genius love of Brainiac 5

        Brainiac 5 thought of everything

he could think of Supergirl except what he was going to say

        to Supergirl

Brainiac 5 Archives the News of the World That Was

At these crosswords and crossworlds I first scan then scry.
The curve and cure of the letter *S*. Pressed to reminders,

eight blank pages of your dear diary absorb the taut trace
of your superscript. Reports of your feats meet and end

in newsprint, the dull smudge stolen from centuries,
pulp and prose, month thin as moth. Your photo only

uniform, just gray and grained until fingerprint close,
a cluster and blur of coal prepressured, postured, rote.

Once you engaged me with carbon, compressed your fist
to palm a perfectly patterned diamond, hardened to beauty.

Each line arcs, irregular. Your signature is a singular mark.
From your notes I know your eye was more poignant than needle,

your ear always amending echo. Therefore I play, as conversation,
the pressings of your hands, which in touching me will call

forth columns of pure fact, actuarial taxonomies, memory
not mine, just sheer reportage and evidence of exploit adorned

with the funneled ink of photograph. Divine, this writing's light.
We derive from the bitter print of tree rings, they who speak

by reminder, who once claimed taste and text but now simply say *then*.
What was news yesterday, new yesterday, ten years by ten years by ten.

Sun Boy / Dirk Morgna of Earth / Superradiance

hey, hotshot, effuse phosphorescent

your good mood purls away gloom

hot-tempered god

always a charmer

well hello ladies

tawny and tawdry

within every charismatic waits a hateful flare

you flirt

cliché in a clinch

golden boy

too hot to touch

touché

the light of the sun

falls equally on everyone

Shrinking Violet / Salu Digby of Imsk / Diminution

once teased and meek

downfallen dust

always underfoot

merely *-ette* for *et uri*

she rises to the occasion

even if easy to miss

once beneath notice

an underestimated threat

now stung and spoiling for a fight

shy soldier in violent bloom

mote is a matter of perspective:

little or distant?

when she returns to normal size

you've grown less in her eyes

Bouncing Boy / Chuck Taine of Earth / Elasticity

soda jerk succumbed to sticky sweet

justifiably jolly

fat & sassy

ballistic boy who plays all the angles

boy enough for two

flagrantly inflated

a lot to work with

a marrying man

Chuck, you're nothing *but* a center of gravity

elastic, incorrigible

cannot be discouraged

butt of every joke

but heroic, too

he's rubber and you're glue

Ultra Boy / Jo Nah of Rimbor / Assortment of superpowers

consider choice / you cannot have everything
at least not all at once / *either* or *or* but never *and*
a hard call for a boy more better than bright / more quick than witted
sequential, so second best / ayup deputy
overrated idiot / undervalued valiant
gets lost & freaks out / *let me check with Phantom Girl first, O.K.?*
choose invulnerability, Jo / it's always the safe way to go

Mon-El / Lar Gand of Daxam

a mighty man / suffused with a thousand years of sadness
he saw it all / phantom zoned for attenuated centuries
somehow haughty *and* humble / benign but also numb
sturdy in his grandeur / sober
lead limited / optimal wanderer
gifted / afflicted
given to nightmares / his quality's apologetic

Matter-Eater Lad / Tenzil Kem of Bismoll / Superdigestion

you'd be surprised how useful it is / to find everything to your taste
he can keep anything down / consumer of malice or metal or miracle
his gullet's furious furnace / happy appetite
Matter-Eater Lad can turn anything / into more Matter-Eater Lad
"waste not, want not!" / smart mouth
give him a moment to digest that / mad with hunger
flatly palatable / *are you gonna eat that?*

What to Expect: Earth on Less than 10 Mega-Credits a Day

Even though this entire planet is overrun with tourists, let's take a hover tour of New Metropolis, the core of which the ancients called New York.

It was relatively tiny, but now includes the whole of the Eastern Seaboard. The Old Boston sector, in particular, is known for its sprightly nightlife.

Behold! The famed skyways of New Metropolis, where you can see the latest in Earth fashions on aerial parade!

That we may rise over our city grid's Q-section, its arch edifice, sheer stone and plassteel, titanet towers glitter stitched with prism.

It eradicates the night sky, lit like infinite candles that gutter but never go out, a city on the hill that sits at the bottom of a well of worlds.

Every resident works hard and happily and without need, for the hundred million citizens make this, make themselves, make science and light.

And here, the Metropolis-Neo-Tokyo core tube terminal! Cut through the mantle of the earth, no layovers, no waiting!

And from there, only a quick jaunt to the wonders of the Hong Kong Spaceport, which receives daily freight and travelers from dozens of planets!

The All-Earth Aesthetics Council has preserved monuments of our past, a long wall of brick, tremendous. But wait until you see Yangtzopolis.

Element Lad / Jan Arrah of Trom / Transmutation

lonely lad	the last mendicant
close to magical	a joiner and a breaker
rearranger	memorious monk
who could turn everything into everything else	no master no mixture
penultimately powerful	he sees what could be
maker of isotope and alloy	our moony ally
infinitely transformative	periodically divine

Light Lass / Ayla Ranzz of Winath / Cancels gravity

who can resist her	a twin sister
innocent, elevated	but readily depressed
sweeter than helium	effortful when uplifting
all buoyantly belligerent	*what's up Light Lass?*
up	points away from the center of the earth
sacrificed lightning for this	mass absent compass
when clouds float we call them clouds	when clouds fall we call them rain

Dream Girl / Nura Nal of Naltor / Precognition

your twilit pause	your comma a deliberate coma
your decisions clinical	faint away, pretty lady
your inevitable conscience	I ought I should
sleep ambitious insomniac	all bedsides beside
brassy Cassandra	glossy with froth
how can you refuse to look	if your eyes are already closed
stay? go?	do you really want to know

18

"The Condemned Legionnaires!"

ADVENTURE COMICS #313, OCTOBER 1963

Here is the saga of the Girl of Steel's struggle

first everything goes dark on fainting Light Lass

then Saturn Girl suddenly sick and Shrinking Violet too

stricken scarlet, all

even Night Girl the Substitute Hero

so the boys stuff the gals in an autopilot space bubble

to hasten them to Quarantine World

(shuffleboard and fruit juice and big maternal nurses whose stray gazes

administer all the curative wavelengths)

(who needs them anyway, girls who can be everywhere, girls
who can get in your hair, girls who can walk through walls, girls
who can *read minds*)

BUT THEN SATAN GIRL STRIKES!!

The boys rebuff her demand for admission

what can one girl do anyway?

even clad head to toe in plum near-black

to supplant the fragile powers, the *trop femme?*

oh she'll show *them*

she'll shred steel to pulp to put them in their place

but the Kids and Lads have christened Supergirl honorary leader

and then there's fisticuffs

it's girl-on-girl

Satan *hates* Super to the cost of trees and boulders

their catfight trashes the landscape

Kara presumes her nemesis a Kryptonian (for she's fierce)

but this Satan Girl laughs off even green K!!

Supergirl's at a loss—afraid

48 hours left to save the superheroines sickened crimson

but Satan Girl persists

zap her with antiandroid gas guns to nil effect

smash her with asteroids and earn irritation

until finally Kara calls in the Legion of Super-Pets

to subdue the villainess

who is she, what's her name?

she unmasks her only to find a second Supergirl

surly under lead-lined leather

oh red kryptonite unpredictable, that severed Supergirl in twine

good girl, bad girl, *both*

one independent id with only her secrets

to supplant her superego

if you had two days to replace yourself would you win your friends again

or deceive them?

address your original essence or erase it?

"It would have been wonderful to live my own life but it's over"

48 hours—a lost weekend, then

see Satan Girl elapse

into Supergirl's skin only to leave her sinister suit

gunmetal body of lingerie underwritten with lead

who can judge her for wanting to live?

poor Satan Girl, forgiven sinner.

"The Menace of Dream Girl!"

ADVENTURE COMICS #317, FEBRUARY 1964

Saturn Girl's a stickler for protocol

she summons all far-flung Legionnaires for meeting

calling all Legionnaires, she's a re-minder

so we sit and sit still

for readings of the Constitution

(clause 6, subclause 3 requires that every Legionnaire use

language learning machines to blah blah)

Mon-El maintains perfect posture

Triplicate Girl nearly falls asleep

finally the new applicants arrive

SIZZLING SUNS!

that Dream Girl's dreamy all right!

the boys go all googly, so *thank God for Saturn Girl*

prissy, proper, impatient

"I'm *sorry*, but *dreaming* isn't a *superpower*"

but the boys, smitten, sweaty, overrule her

and Nura dreams TERRIBLE MENACE:

eggs that hatch reeking beasts

Metropolis Spaceport blown to bits

When the vote comes it falls along gender lines

yea boys and nay ladies

but crises wait not for courting

the iron curtain of time

persists but by now Dreamy's an unmanageable bitch

she mission accompanies Lightning Lass, who "somehow"

loses her powers

It doesn't stop there, either

Dream Girl's read the rules rightly

she's suddenly Clause Queen

speaking Law French and all those stupid subclauses

she takes us out one by one

she uses the Vondra Aurora to turn us into superinfants.

who knows what motivates pretty people

                                    but the boys are surely sore about it now
                          yet it turns out Nura had dreamed an unclear dream

she saw us die and sought to save us

(for how can harm come to Legionnaires-no-longer?)

                                in the end it's a compromise

          sorry for the confusion, she says

          won't you reapply, Star Boy asks

and Dream Girl says *maybe later.*

                            But she's *Dream Girl*. She *knew*

          even then. Unfair, her future

                                    that once was ours.

What to Expect: Future Ecology

Cities sprawl, artful, without happenstance.

Because urban planning has infinite reach, they are beautiful, choral, colorful as oceans.

Beautiful, but sterile.

Still, no suburbs, only cityscapes.

Clean, neat.

Zones once considered inhospitable revert to naked states: deserts unfold without interruption, seas surge—fresh, unfished—jungles mutate to keenly shaded greens, plains rustle.

Every acre of once-wild will be primeval, floral, faunal.

The globe, a garden.

"Revolt of the Girl Legionnaires!"
ADVENTURE COMICS #326, NOVEMBER 1964

a single scene

sinuous but also a snapshot

      six women dance in the clubhouse

      fearless, cheerful

                  what's the celebration for?

        since adventure always ends in revelation

                    let's start there for once

      once upon a time on the planet Femnaz (yes)

there were men and women

      women armored in brushed steel and helmeted in red

        women who fought in arenas

          men who wore lavender robes

        men held themselves aloof

    while the warrior-women held them in contempt

      especially when they tsk'd the women's moon worship

    which the men feared might crack the moon in half

so into space arks the men were shuffled

after which Azura the queen of the planet hypnotizes the girl Legionnaires she wants them to betray the boys before betrayed by

but here's how they went about matters:

Light Lass kisses Element Lad

Triplicate Girl kisses Invisible Kid
            kisses Brainiac 5
            kisses Cosmic Boy

Saturn Girl says *kiss me Superboy*

Chameleon Boy tries to kiss Supergirl

Phantom Girl lets Star Boy kiss her

                                        is it really that easy?

neither the romance nor the betrayal last

        it turns out the women of Femnaz *did* crack their moon in half

                and contrite Azura wipes the minds she's washed

        she had hypnotized the girls into hatred

            she had tricked the girls into sinister kisses

                she had capitalized on adolescent hope

        she had primed them for primacy

                                trick girls

                                gimmick girls

                                whipsmart girls

        whom no one had to make dance.

27

Let's start with superstring, a theory of asynchronous information, so that what is is what does: vibrating, symphonic supersymmetry. Add mass supersaturated to supergravity, and then scale up to superclusters of super-galaxies, aglow with supergiant stars, syncopated with supernovae. What music have we missed? Can we dance to the tune as we play it? The regions between, where we live. We feel still because we speed. The superior planets refer just to those farther from where you are. Superlunary, what you dream of when you look into what you wrongly call the sky.

Signed,
Brainiac 5

"The Weddings that Wrecked the Legion!"

ADVENTURE COMICS #337, OCTOBER 1965

has Brainiac 5 finally flipped his lid??

he's nattering on about *Plan R*

Phantom Girl and Ultra Boy canoodle and nuzzle

Brainy's peeved to say the least

does no one care about Plan R?

so in steps Saturn Girl

he admires her

but she's sweet on Lightning Lad!

paired lovers moon about the museum

"Only you stood up for me, Phantom Girl!"

"How could you ever love a boy with a robot arm?"

unbeknown to all secret agents who watch and listen and wonder:

What is Plan R??

the agents kidnap Saturn Girl who summons Lightning Lad

seeing suddenly how empty life would be without her, Garth proposes

and Imra says *yes* and then they quit

just like that

for there are rules in the Legion Code and these are they

Ultra Boy and Phantom Girl follow too.

Four Legionnaires lost

thought Brainy was out of sorts before? Holy cats!!

"Your cold emotional computer mind can't comprehend what love is!"

Et tu, Saturn Girl?

Still, she says she's sorry

but B5 just rolls his eyes and seeks to fill the ranks

meanwhile, singleton Mon-El is missing his married pals

adventures and events commence

the secret agents seek membership under false pretense and fake disguise

SIZE LAD! BLACKOUT BOY! MAGNETIC KID!

but they're foiled easily enough

"they" usually are foiled easily enough

that was Plan R the whole time

but Saturn Girl and Brainy were in on it together!

a relief like Shakespeare

weddings and order restored

but Brainiac notes that since the chaplain was a robot

the weddings are actually fake

Quick thinking, Brainiac 5!!

But now Garth & Imra & Jo & Tinya have had a taste

the clock's ticking

see, Brainiac, that's the problem

you're always giving them ideas.

"The Sacrifice of Kid Psycho!"
SUPERBOY #125, DECEMBER 1965

Dear Mr. and Mrs. Opral,

Does your baby have a giant head?

Even for a baby?

there's good news

he is likely a mutant with extraordinary mental powers

however, your world will be destroyed and you with it

because the more extraordinary the offspring

the more likely your world is to die

but you will make sure your large-headed, large-hearted son will escape

to safety in a rocket ship

he will do good, he will wear a turban, he will call himself Kid Psycho

every time he does something awesome

he will slice a year off his life.

Rest assured

this is the kind of boy the Legion keeps in reserve

even though you brought him up right

all your boy will want to do is die

don't feel bad

after all, what is life worth

if you must sacrifice your youth to save it?

Brainiac 5 Pitches a Hypothesis Fit

No one is only ever clever. No form is merely function.
An experiment isn't a test. How high do you think IQ can go?

Count on your alien fingers. If necessary go to your toes.
I'll memorize pi for awhile. It's fine, I'm fine, why do you ask?

I am a genius trapped in a bottle. Do I exasperate? So do you.
You are inadequate to even crap mathematics. I want you to think

about how I feel but you cannot think and I do not feel. Oh well.
Ditch the idiom, chum. My mood's as considered as my diction.

I gave you rings with which to fly while I sit still
in this industrial grove, alone, smartening steel, asymptotic.

I take incomparable care, while you planet smash and grasp.
Who isn't my patient? I do not acknowledge anything latent,

I haven't the patience. Go to play, go to space. I've robots
to plot. Immersion in emptiness destroys distance. Distance begs

limit. But you cannot get it, the limit I cannot admit. Let me
tell you about a dream I have. The New Metropolis train accelerates

down its magnetic track while I'm held fast, point punctuation
on the high-speed line. I deduce its blueprint in my head and shunt

the momentum into exploded view. Its engineering releases.
Forward momentum radiates neatly, parts part, A decouples from B.

Disassembled, it waits in my mind, done and unknown then known and undone.
I understand it to bits and pieces. Do you know what this portends?

I know the dream train to every article, adjustment, and fault.
I know the real train just as well. So tell me: why doesn't it halt?

"Computo the Conqueror!"

when comes the revolution

all that was once under will lord it over

first you were master then mammal then meat

when comes the machine revolution

neither robot nor computer but *robot computer*

it takes away everything that makes its inventor special

(who makes this monster??)

(Brainiac 5, who else??)

his sophistication engine versus organic intelligence

the more loquacious Computo becomes the more colloquial Brainy gets

as if he could outtalk an encyclopedia

to resist Computo the Conqueror

this is to sling mud at a gunfight

maybe Brainy thinks *the answer is human feeling*

but then the machine orchestrates the sound of every emotion at once

awful noise of sob and scream and laugh and gasp

this is serious

did that thing just kill a Triplicate Girl?

and Brainy knows the cure for having overthought:

overthinking

take *that*, you heap of bolts

the problem of the problem solver solved

but now we're down to a Duo Damsel

and Brainy, even you can't blame those who wonder

how long you can solve more problems than you create.

"The Super-Stalag of Space!"

ADVENTURE COMICS #344, MAY 1966

the warden desires the traitor made naked

   it's a habit true to a type

      here's a prison planet for heroes

         but the boggle-eyed guards sequester heroines

   in separate pens

         the warden is running out of teens to torture

under such pressure who *wouldn't* crack

         the warden tried unspooling Brainy's brain

   but how hard can *that* be

                  his blond forelock unlocked

      HIM the green boy cried it's HIM

            named the traitor named their terror

& the gayest superhero in the United Planets leapt about the barracks

   like a weightless wizard, which he was

            he sprang on thighs coiled against gravity

   purple and white, the orchid blur of him

   such a man to make even Brainy look macho

fled into floral fields and for fuck's sake lily pads

one of which opened

carnal, vulval, unsubtle—

and ate him up

tragic, but also a warning

aw, warden, we just wanted to teach that spring-heeled sissy a lesson

meanwhile Matter-Eater Lad is the tunnel king of this prison narrative

cheeky, full of stone

struck down on the other side of the fence

it looks like curtains for the kids

then rescue comes via some accident

firing squad beams bounce off invincible chests

somehow M-E lad concludes as punitively fat

for all these penalized it is Superboy and Mon-El who return

to wreak vengeance

lean on, fattened heroes, filthy heroes

brainwashed and bullied and bunk bedded these long weeks

they append and suffix us with boy

but we are men.

Ferro Lad / Andrew Nolan of Earth / Superferrous

our humble human shield
turned his birth curse
armor up, son
superheated engulfed golem
or a guaranteed goner who went well
every gesture hewn
mirror chrome under which an ugly boy

almost equal to his anxiety
to serve and protect
annihilated iron gone to gas
his exit a glory-flourish, foolish
statue-who-moves
his sheer mask metallic
befanged, beneath

Karate Kid / Val Armorr of Earth / Superkarate

best barehanded
the aperture a dragon
constant practice
unbelievably tasked
callus masterful
able but cannot end well
righteous in his pride

two hands almost clasped
apprentice of fracture & crack
smooth because you have something to prove
he builds himself from scratch
body artist improbable agile &
your blisters shut into sandpaper
ride your beatings bravely, baby

Princess Projectra of Orando / Superillusionist

she sure fooled you
illustrious distraction
a complement of conjure
look again
conjure wright
imperial pigments titanium white
regal faker

she points at what isn't there
illustrated air
each image abjury & injury
tell me what you see
her right's divine
a medium a seer who modifies sight
old-fashioned fashioner

"The Doomed Legionnaire!"
ADVENTURE COMICS #353, FEBRUARY 1967

this is the most important thing that will ever happen to us

      when the most important thing that will ever happen to you begins

    you don't know

        which isn't to say it starts as something small

in this case we know immediately the threat:

          pink candyfloss that eats suns

             a clotted cotton cloud without a sky

            unless all of space counts as sky

                  the sun eater has no mind

    there's nothing for us to trick or bludgeon or convince

    so we do something we never do

               we ask for help

but everyone is busy or selfish or despairing

      or else can't read our plea

      (though etched in flare visible for millions of miles)

    pressed for time we cut a deal with the Fatal Five

immunity for aid

we compromise, we plan, we fail

and finally Ferro Lad just flies a bomb into the pink beast

into diffusion he soars

into tendrils and voracious glittering candydust

Ferro Lad incandesces and will never come back

all those lives we are always saving

of course death occurred to us

you could call it our antimotivator

but only now do we know what is to be destroyed.

Silver

Ferro Lad Memorial Action Figure

SOLDIER BOY

Happy as a waltz with you in my palm.
Jarhead, miniature metal marine, heroic force
since 2959, how do you come in your mutant
shine to the utter jungle of my backyard?
Legionnaire, I flung you like a grenade, all heft
and lantern jaw, all intent, flung you at mud,
which only yielded bubble, flung you at birds,
scarlet roped from long, tricky scarves.
Nothing could shake the mask from your shiny shell,
or empty your innards of iron, chrome cast
all the way to skin. How happy I was
with your ideals of sacrifice, your martyring,
your faithless marriage to terrible tasks.
No iris in the iron orbit of your skull.
No hair saved but that combed by magnets,
when you were molten red, just born,
missionless without me.

FUTURE MAN

Your weight greater than a stack of drawings,
each page a frame of colonial fun.
Stupid cloisonné helmet, white
that could be chipped, stupid silver-blue
suit that held the gleam of your mutant muscle.
I cut you open with a hacksaw and found
iron, opened your absurd weight to vacuum,
left you die again and again and again.
Transsuited for space, yet you sank even in tubs,
refused rust though stranded in sewers.
The hard minor bulk of you was my every hope.

Why, if I am ugly, can I not alchemize to isotope?
A red handkerchief quartered with ball bearings
barely slows you in your descent from my roof.
Squat man, hero type, so weighty.
What is it, deep in the heart of the sun,
that wants you so near.

Brainiac 5's Very Bad Valentine

Argo extruded you, a seed, summer personified. You were a private girl
and a private god. Cousin, but unkissed. A golden apparatus.

Your measure more molybdenum than mere might: you proved your myth
with evidence of exploit and archetype, you proved fiction remiss.

Underearth you disgorged even greater prehistories, arks, and excaliburs.
Your pirouettes spiraled granite. At induction we recalled my ancestor

Brainiac Prime, whose revolt against the computer tyrants of Colu
allowed my evolutions. On the way he flattened your cousin a few times

and abused your spun-out hometown, gone Argo, glass asteroid.
Your death was the news of nine hundred years and a great computation:

how we met. I made basic shapes and bobbed them on eons. I solved
time. It wasn't hard: just geometry and capacity and thinking I could.

I built a beacon, a bubble, a cube to invite you, replace your orphanage.
Traveled time clings to your fingers: rainbow, the kids call it,

though it is neither precipitate nor arc, even if nausea to navigate.
As distraction I built houseboys that murdered girls in triplicate.

If I lost many of my very many magnificent marbles know I saved more days
than I misplaced. Once pulsed in your invulnerable wrist veins aglow

with sun-platelets from which daylight ensued. Unstoppered Supergirl,
loosened. Your posthumous successes toxify my headspace, my holospace.

Your anniversary annuls my deterioration. Calculating, Saturn Girl
calls me: I am a genius and it is thus incumbent upon me to calculate,

to deliberate: I locate you to decimal point and pluck your uniquely
sunny and selfless 20th-century decency for my own abject embraces.

All this sent from my laboratories to ask: go with me, stop time,
unscroll the parchment of superheroics, destatue, die less, Be Mine.

Sarcastic to the point of being supercilious: guilty. But imagine if at rest your excess thoughts outclassed endless banks of supercomputers; if you were, in fact, above computability. What others might mistake for arrogance would simply be id tainted by a requisite abundance of supergo. It takes a lot of discipline to keep complexity in check so that it doesn't devolve into superiority complex. The stress is immense. Sometimes the torsion coils superhelical. And sometimes what I superintend I instead superordinate; what I wish to supervise I supervene. The words I use to account for this constitute a superstratum language; I'm talking myself down. The superposition principle states that every linear system must be an additive one: the stories I tell. In explaining them, I explain us, in explaining us, I explain myself.

Sincerely,
Brainiac 5

What to Expect: Gadget Catalog

After the cashiering of amalgonite refineries, comfort is secured by fusion powerspheres, for which there is no black market.

The Joneses keep up with *Worldwide 3-D News*, sponsored by the ultimate road vehicle: the Astrovette 8000!

We are linked via visiphone; we adduce the aberrant via crime computer; we keep track of our cohort with the Monitor Board.

Yet how often do fiends speak the words "prepare the ray cannon"—

Rip-rays to shear through steel, antitron guns, retrorifles, and solar stunners, energo shields.

War by other means is conducted on Weber's World, a huge metal moon.

We deposit telepathic plugs in your ear.

We slide your transsuit on, one leg at a time.

We will upgrade our jet packs to flight belts; we will upgrade our flight belts to flight rings, even more economical means of flight—gleaming, heraldic, and characterized by ease of use.

When misfortune befalls us, we give thanks for plasticasts and medikits, the satellite hospitals of Medicus One.

If even greater misfortune befalls us, we give thanks for detention spheres and mentoscanners.

We are rewarded for our heroism with all forms of intergalactic specie, including the metal-eating beasts of Rojunn, none of which we need.

As we set aside molecular glue guns, as we remove our antitelepathy helmets, rest in these battery beds.

We visit the Carey Interplanetary Library and rifle through its dusty holotapes.

We loiter in the Hall of Infinite Knowledge.

We store abstract art graven in light in our tesseract closet.

Even Computo will suffer gradual domestication; even Computo will bring us fruit juice.

And don't forget the Miracle Machine, sitting in our basement.

It turns thoughts into reality. We do not think about it.

Instructions for the Use of Telepathic Plug

If the Fatal Five surprise you in the singles' district of New Metropolis, then there will opalesce the optic enchantment, the silent Emerald Eye of Ekron, rotating to the bidding of its empress. Then Tharok the half-man bisected robot, shaved head stitched into skull and shell, and black-profiled Mano, whose palm is obliteration. If there is Tharok then there will be two-fingered Validus, his braincase lucid and lurid, mentation ozone of his terrible toddler's rage. If the Fatal Five then the masked Persuader and his atomic ax, splitter of atoms, thinking thing, which requires its own prison.

place snugly within the ear

"The School for Super-Villains!"

You cannot know whom you are going to annoy

and accidents do happen

cops and robbers is all fun and games

yes, until someone gets clipped in the throat with a laser beam

he's called Tarik (the Mute)

you would be bitter, too

if you had to have a robot follow you around and verbalize for you

the point is that bitter draws bitter

and we've done some damage, too

inspired lads and lasses to apply

girls and boys who came to us in hope

what about that kid who could make himself flat as a sheet?

and the girl with the telekinetic hair?

the more popular we grow the more we have to say no

is it any wonder those whose hopes we dashed would make their own
ill clique?

still, empathy only goes so far

it doesn't matter how disappointed you are

you can't just turn Colossal Boy's parents to glass

we don't blame *him*

he only sold us out to save someone else

yes, he could have asked us for help

big dummy

but we don't take any pride in kicking your asses in

we also don't know how much our mercy can sting.

What to Expect: The Legion Code

From first principles we must be young, brave, unique, disciplined.

And hence the Legion Code, which prohibits murder even in self-defense unless the Legionnaires in question are threatened by the Time Trapper, in which case we'll just have to think about it.

And let it be known that each of us must be unique, and let it be known that the married of us shall be banished, as one with the murderers in the lengths of the Legion Code; aye, redundancies and murderers and marrieds alike.

Let us hold the almost worthy and the almost ready in reserve and christen a Legion Academy situated on Montauk Point, from which shall issue proto-Legionnaires, guided under the tutelage of the Bouncing Boy and the Duo Damsel, she who was once Triplicate Girl.

Thus we authorize the Substitute Legion, whose ranks shall swell with those we reject, be they Stone Boys or Chlorophyll Kids, inspired by our awesomeness, our excellence, the elegance of our extraordinary outfits.

So as to ever improve we pledge to continue our scientific education when time allows, when we aren't pursuing space pirates, when we aren't out on the town.

So as to maintain good health, no one of us may complete more than five (5) space missions in a row, for that would increase our risk of space sickness, of going mad, of becoming cowardly, of committing murder, of getting married.

If for any reason we must resign membership, we agree to have erased from our memory all rules, regulations, codes, and secrets.

Yet, until that time, we obey.

Instructions for the Use of Telepathic Plug

If Universo, expatriated Green Lantern, father of Rond Vidar, perfects hypnotic rhetoric at the council of the Science Police, his monocle most central, concentric, ripple willed. If the constabulary sleep in his dreaming.

If the lovers Grimbor the Chain Maker and Charma caramelize mischief malice. Supersadist from the asteroid orphanage and her macho masochist, leather clad, his muscle medieval. If her fetish focuses on acquisition his limp will will submit.

If Mordru undoes the Sorcerer's World and eldritch infants commence. If planets transpose then alternate realities and timelines untwine. If reserve membership maculates.

heed the alarm signal, Legionnaires

"Twelve Hours to Live!"

ADVENTURE COMICS #378, MARCH 1969

worst birthday ever, Brainiac 5!!

one minute you are playing the lumna organ

(a gift from your chums who groove to those crazy tunes)

(*of course* you've had *piano lessons*)

and the next everyone is toasting your health

and the next uh oh you have all been poisoned

how paranoid is paranoid enough?

now you each have twelve hours to live:

Superboy does deeds because he has no imagination

Duo Damsel plays Ping-Pong with her pop

while Duo Damsel plays chess with her mom

Karate Kid picks a fight x Fatal Five

Projectra goes to see a movie and feeds pigeons in the park

I can't even tell you what happens next

it's too stupid

let's just say you're saved by *something beyond*

if we must have lessons and morals then this:

it all starts pleasantly

whatever in any instance "it" is

and then life goes on

or is it *but then life goes on*

or is it *or*

or is it *if.*

Shadow Lass / Tasmia Mallor of Talok VIII / Superdarkness

there are some things from which you cannot hide if eyes widen unwilled
she's oblivion to others tainted and tinted
terror's tourney in her irradiant radius jet-black beckoner
her ink absolute blue ladle out the shade
that peculiar Spartan darkness womb warm, unwitnessed
little miss mysterious simple as antisun yet subtle as gas
ask our Shadow Lass are shadows shadowless

Chemical King / Condo Arlik of Phlon / Supercatalyst

catalytic, kid unfastened bonds coalesce into chemical nets
molecular action unravels recumbent stutter as electron speed shudders
now iron is rust now ocean is oxygen
you adopt kingship in the company of children watch this trick
you're a killer you advance engines to decay
who wants your compounded company your transformative tang
instant organic erosion your only heroic affect

Timber Wolf / Brin Londo of Zuun / Superacrobat

passive-aggressive dolt sniffing his way through the bewilderness
functionless without a fight he gnaws doggedly
all instinct and appetite tamed by ladies
eager boy easy boy one moment he turns his face away
the next his eyes ruby rage the shift comes growl, aroused
held captive in his own claws his touch rough, he admires animal
a sad façade his face parade

Sense-Maps of the United Planets

Braal / at dawn / wasp rings pucker the binding force / oh
these iron beasts beset us, Lord / their horns and ferrous filings
let us make magnetic / let us repulse and click
settler's electro weft, woven

Disheveled Winath and her lightning crows / the labor of the sheaves
forever undone / rain abrasions / your perfect granaries and gametes
twin androgynes all and freckled

Titan, imperial strokes and strides / horizons loom at your windows
adept your offspring bathe in one mind / severe sexes of Titan
regal preserve of privacy / moon-fingers picking apart pathogens

Ales and alleys of Rimbor / inkparlors and whores / chromatic bouquet
evening scent lays Rimbor suspended between doorframe and city scene
scoundrels

Earth / buoyed in a polymer screen / the planet's prophylactic
seven sprawling cities / whole continents preserved for parks
diplomatically diverse / capital planet

Naltor-that-dreams / mercurial moldings and sleep sweat
precognition glistens / your pillows and parted lips
platinum and probable /come to bed with us

Krypton / buckled under her own majestic freight / organless at the end
adorned over every inch / mathematical maternities / her womb cracked
dead of her delivery

little sister Daxam / godhands tucked in surgeon's gloves
engineers of immature / the pristine garden cultures of Daxam
shattered / her seedlings spread throughout the worlds
done in by base / exiled to airlessness

Cargg multiplicative / fashionable girls shudder into thirds
subtle schizophrenics / always boxes shaken loose from boxes
mirrorless but mindful

The anachronisms of Orando / craggy king and stony castle
ungoverned rains / monarchial and matter of fact
suit of armor and shield still
stand in every able man's house

Infinitesimal Imsk's shrinking season / transport for tourists
gigantic architecture / transpiring underfoot even now
perspective here burgeons and billows
falling-down world, misplaced, minor

Bgtzl, which is barely / phantom phase-shifted to mists
export of black and ashy intangerines / Bgtzl, which passes through you
which eludes

Colu is / a sleep negation / impedimentary flesh hosts
curved corridors / hypercognitive and effectively ageless
supreme intellects of Colu / instinct unsubstantiated
in its circuit-cities

That caves of Talok IV dwindle to gasses of impenetrable jet
her chalk-blue heroines / nocturne tuned and martial
dwellers in the cliffs set themselves against dwellers of the plains
effacing shades, her unlight, her curious dark

Xerox / sorcerers' world / imaginary / its landmasses magic
they shimmer and drip, they slither and blink
all illusion / inheritable errors / rock wreathed in unreason
ever unfolding and uncertain

Durla, about which everything / clans and cults and customs
rigid for the regulation of pure shape / molten membership
irradiated, ruinous fluids / forbidden, this place
its soil face and its ovum oceans

and murdered Trom / pillage for plunder / leadened and leavened
alchemical legend / lost monks and lost meditations / empty of elementals
her seas shout / her salts foam and form
the salt of her seas
follows suit

Bronze

What to Expect: Fashion Forward

Hell, in the spring of blooming youth and with the gift of magical fabrics even that butterball Bouncing Boy looks good enough to eat: he fits in a slimming black-and-blue jumpsuit.

Everything's gone around, everything's come around.

Thus the thirty-second iteration of the bouffant and the go-go boot.

And therefore the cape of Princess Projectra of Orando, for its length and its suppleness, and its adherence to her royal declivities and convexitudes.

Likewise the flared collar of her consort Val Armorr and his pectoral and abdominal muscles and his navel, magnificent.

For naught need protection nor support and thus all indulge utter erotica.

Witness Cosmic Boy only glove'd and bootie'd, Cosmic Boy now presenting maximum clavicle.

Witness Tyroc, whose white onesie erupts into a butterfly collar, whose breast is barely contained by golden rope.

Taketh in thy waistcoat, tucketh in thy lace.

This year's style is the style of every year previous, for the 30th century cannot tell history from utility from frivolity.

Whither the zipper on this thing? Wherefore zipper when our suits are skintight, seal smooth, cleaved to fit us at the apex of our fitness?

Even modest Light Lass refuses to wear pants.

Element Lad has silver snaps all up his back back back.

Timber Wolf Loves Light Lass

The lovers: his all-Latin omnicom
sits, blush red by the rust of his archaic lamps.
    His lexicon stretches to admit her.

Meager mattress, pitcher of water.
Light Lass slips lightly through window and door.
    Her impatience with his ancient—

the woman actually covers her mouth
when she laughs. Simple scent of cooking haunts the HQ,
    touches the lemon juice in his hair.

The modern chef's hands slice, superprecise.
He furies a teacup and she pauses its gravity again.
    He throws a second, she stakes the same.

Neither look: neither need. But they do.
The manners of his multiformed face: his half-feral fangs.
    He does not know what he should look like.

She remains unfamiliar with his physicality.
Sex between them, yes, but not because it's best to pretend.
    Simply seamless with what they are.

She flings him out the window, then.
Superacrobatic, he reaches for the flagpole. His lateral
    gravity defeats, for a moment, her vertical.

They fit, neat and abraxas, like her
legs fixed around his waist as he steps backward
    across their quarters, her weight welded.

He leaves chalk where the balls
of his feet have touched, easy with her freight.
　　　Newly intimate, familiars.

　　　His calluses scratch against her,
their costumes mingle, the sunlight goes all moody and flat
　　　over the alabaster of New Metropolis.

　　　She places her fingers in the wolf's mouth.
It's no story: perhaps they spend the night uninterrupted,
　　　their skintight selfish.

　　　They fall, and frequently, and have learned
when to ease in collapse, when to snap tight as a sheet
　　　pulled taut. Peace is to never touch:

　　　Float or fly over the certain ground, survive
via sequence of skips, tabletop to a roof sticky with sun.
　　　The peace your world has known cannot last.

　　　These words broken by Timber Wolf's book.
Theirs is an introductory course based on ancient tongues.
　　　No alphabet holds such action in't.

Wildfire / Drake Burroughs of Earth / Superenergy

hell's lasting backfire

blaze & rage

bodiless braggart

a spectacular accident's acerbic aftermath

lacking a face

he's mastered the expressive gesture

irritable, incorporeal, unstable

yet impressively able

a seething son of a bitch

held together with will

the spirit that moves

rude fuel

for whom the suit

makes the man

Tyroc / Troy Stewart of Marzal Island / Super-weird yells

polyglottal

hummable human

driven by injustice barking mad

out loud basso bellower

vocal whoop and holler

a whole audible hubbub

whisperer & whistler

you make him want to scream

range as deep as it is wide

shout it out enraged,

enranged

he's clearing his throat

listen up, everybody

he has something to say

Dawnstar / Dawnstar of Starhaven / Supertracking

she always knows where you've been

disillusioned muse

dismissive of distance

oblivious to open space

happiest in hard vacuum

actually as fast as light

carelessly pretty girl

bitchy as her oblivious beauty

dreadful, withering witness

she can locate a needle in infinite space

trace strung to target

she cannot get lost

she can find anything and she wants nothing

keep up if you can

"One-Shot Hero!"

SUPERBOY #195, JUNE 1973

here's a sad story:

Drake Burroughs has an industrial accident

no, wait, Drake Burroughs *is* an industrial accident

        a propulsion engineer engulfed in antienergy

            on the negative side: no more body

    on the positive: every power imaginable

      he comes to us too various, he makes us redundant

     but what else would a young man do in such circumstances

          but petition for Legion membership?

what else is a young man to do but wait for another industrial accident?

              this is the 30th century

agricultural and industrial are interchangeable

and on Manna V

       ("It provides food for billions everywhere!")

   blackmailers have unleashed an eating machine

it's big

68

bigger than Colossal Boy at his biggest

the team is doomed

when Drake Burroughs

stowaway

uses the one power no other Legionnaire has

all his antienergy emptied in one big boom

a heroic gesture

here's a sad story

the boy puts his heart into it but (having none)

he cannot put his heart back in.

Brainiac 5 Drops the Plot

Once I got assaulted with psychoactive Preparation L:
Potent chemicals vexed the reason of my mighty mind.

It was bent to tell you of bodies changed into other bodies.
Your bodies are all variants on one body. My privacy was violated.

It made me crazy. I am always doing this, I never do this.
Whatever inside your mind if moved by other than mind

is still mind. Whereas my brain is infinitely divisible
your brain has thirds and threads. My thought is your action.

Your body, in its living, becomes abhorrent; only in death is it worse.
What you know as myth, which once was verse, began with a curse.

Now it's science that goes wrong but once it was gods gone bad,
but in each instance it's always us, we're who we shouldn't trust.

Orpheus. He was believed to be the very best, not least by Orpheus.
He was an augur, a singer. Medicine and music he brought to us.

Like us, he had elaborately able companions and monstrous woes.
Like us, he adventured. Like me, he lost her. You know the rest.

Why did he think he could get her back? Because he knew he could.
Why did he not get her back? Because he did not know he had.

Mind of sap or mind of lightning. Every mind is bent by its body.
Gods were once animals and facts are now gods, wholly haughty.

Because my grip on life is less than tight I bequeath unto us
the facts of my nature. In rending, I render. I always, I never.

"The Hero Who Hated the Legion!"

SUPERBOY #216, APRIL 1976

having solved poverty chronic illness environmental woes & rudeness

explain, then, 30th century

why floats an autonomous island

marvelous Marzal

occupied by radical black separatists

how could you have neglected to mention this?

you've united endless orreries of planets

but here's Science Fiction Liberia

whose lone hero is one angry black man

whose superpower is to raise his voice

Tyroc wants to know where the hell you've been

he also wants you to get the hell out

either way he's got a point that is lost on you

"He's really bitter!" you say

and then give him the speech

just because some of you *are* orange or blue or green

that doesn't mean you can say

"We don't *see* color!"

                              how is it that *you* rescue *him*

              how is it that in rescuing him

                              you pull off his disguise

        which is a whiteface

                              and he says *thank you*

and even looks forward to joining your club?

                    how did you essentialize an *us* from *this*

        how is it that now some of his best friends

        are *you?*

"We Can't Escape the Trap in Time!"

SUPERBOY #223, JANUARY 1977

it's a big galaxy

        something is always going awry

    by now we can make a calculus out of it

        if we don't x then y

where x is something hard and y is something bad

      and because we are always on a clock

why *shouldn't* Superboy just wrap us in his cape

    why shouldn't we break the time barrier

    well *here's* why

      just as walking backward invites accident

time's only supposed to move in one direction

   going the wrong way invites the Time Trapper

   so *this* time is *that* time

        there he is

  all "have supper, won't you, I'm evil"

   this mission is going wrong

    this mission has always gone wrong

73

and now the five time-tossed legionnaires must die

or else the Trapper cannot rule each of infinite alternate futures

his omnicomputer has discerned it so

yet as each of the five fight

their initiatives entwine with the efforts of the others

every moment simultaneous

every movement likewise so

each action's end undone and thereby unstarted

beginning to end

yes it's confusing

all this used to be so easy

bank robbers, space pirates

now we need advanced degrees just to throw a punch

the calculus holds if just

still it's a headache

in conclusion Superboy (at home if out of place)

decides to research the Legion manual

chapter? time travel

author? Brainiac 5

because when it comes to stuff like this, he wrote the book.

Blok of Dryad / Superstone

not *meat*	really truly rocky
thick as a stone because *stone*	gravel voiced
whose literal heart is hard	all one substance, seamless
how's he doing?	well he's scraping by
stolid student of human nature	stalwart gentleman
the more gentle for being less the man	a slowly eroding poet
our foundation reduced to rubble	*aw, Blok* he was thinking it through

Invisible Kid II / Jacques Foccart of Earth / Invisibility

who is wearing the dead man's shoes	sorry, who are you?
number two kid	new kid
the wrong time, the wrong place	he hates capes, he hates space
the opposite of grandiose	a polite Francophone
the closest we ever came to an adult	he does what he has to do
he takes someone else's medicine	he fades from view
he never has much fun	but he fades to the occasion

White Witch / Mysa Nal of Naltor / Spellcaster

pristine	pale as unaltered marble
she's studious, too	modestly utterly smarter than you
library hush	lovely bloodshot
composed, comportment	weapon of last resort
arms folded in sleeves like parchment	her manner an elegant garment
always prepared	she strikes a pose
she hovers ethereal, uncanny	she masters her craft

Orphans

even if anyone remained you could not go home
the world to which you cannot return
because it is empty absent ravaged
legendary

you cannot tell where fell every body
where will fall fragments
where once were families
every orphan is one of many

and many the ways to desolation
for you left in fear of your life
or were sent away in grief
or set yourself to revenge

strays and remainders
last sons and exiles
in a gallery of one of everything
even orphans are only one of many

Polar Boy / Brek Bannin of Tharr / Supercold

naïve	snow-blinded into seeing only the bright side
a former benchwarmer	he left us cold
redeemed reject	regular rule follower once an almost
absolute zero	he focuses, frigid
weather-possessed	finally, finally, little man
the cooler head prevailed	he hopes to be better whether
he lowers the standards	but he carries the flag

Sensor Girl / Projectra of Orando / Supermysterious

she's foolproof	regretful regent
inductress of ignorance	forthcoming as a black sack
affectless	she cannot face us
fuller illusionist	just scary sometimes
blinder, deafener	she stuns foes to dumbness
still regal	never merely a murderer
mild amid riddles	to every question, sensor is the answer

Roll Call Speed Date

I was the head of my class.
I was a world-class ballplayer.
I got attacked by lightning beasts.
Everyone's like this where I come from.
Everyone's like *this* where *I* come from.
No one's left where I come from.
No one else leaves where I come from.
I just got lucky.
I made a potion and drank it.
My parents did this to me.
Everyone's like this where I come from, but less so.
I got locked in a lab by a mad scientist.
Everyone's like this where I come from.
Someone else made a potion and I drank it.
I got swallowed by a space whale.
Everyone's like this where I come from.
Everyone was like this where I came from until a space pirate murdered them.
I got attacked by lightning beasts but then I met Dream Girl.
Um, it's congenital?
I taught myself.
I'm enjoying my royal prerogative.
I'm the last of my matriarchal line.
I'm just special like that, I guess.
My dad experimented on me.
My body was destroyed and this is what's left.
I don't know, I just am.
I'm the best.
I'm the last.
I'm the next.
I'm pretty average, actually.
I'm getting better and better.
We've met before.

Sun Boy Loves Anything that Moves

Some contempt is the honest consequence of talk
about what you do on vacation. In the stories
his friends will tell of him, they will claim
that he would schedule his own funeral
for the uncommon hour of
a light supper of dry cheese and red wine.
Shrewdly, no one will note that he is so handsome
that the dilation of his pupils is sufficient
to establish lust and regret in whole other species.
If this seems all too catty, ask who else would confess
to generating his own mood light.
Who *is* afraid of the dark?
He has slain every lady to whom he ever paid
the slightest attention, even if
they all survived. Death by Sun Boy
causes the heart to beat with a force that can be heard
across a room. A pity, that the burn
follows less quickly than the speed of his light.
Beauty is not what the beautiful despise.

Colossal Boy Loves Shrinking Violet

30th century and girls still hum, inarticulate,
to six strings
in dorm rooms. She's deep as a well,
Imskian, shy there
on the sphere that dwindles like a candle.
His name is Gim-with-a-G Allon because
it's the future
and he fell into a comet's tail, or his spacecraft did,
and that's his origin,
much like that of Thom-with-an-H
Kallor, whose parents'
observation satellite was subject to another celestial trail.
Thom can induce
gravity's pull and increase the mass of objects and Gim
can get real real big.
He's always loved her but even more since she changed
to the new costume
with the black leather thigh-high fold-over boots.
She's a shrinker,
Salu Digby is: irised, down to a hair's width and clinging
to the lip
of her water glass during Legion roll call.
And then one day
she slips into something more comfortable.
No one told
Duplicate Boy, of course, and there was a fight,
and Boys Duplicate and Colossus
tore hell out of the Alps, though you would think Duplicate Boy
would have seen it coming,
what with a name
like Duplicate Boy, and who knows what he saw
with his duplicated X-ray vision,
even if he saw it
from planets away.

Maybe he saw his girl shrink to a mite and dance
in the big man's
inner ear
until the hammer there tripped him dizzy, maybe she swam
up his caudate nucleus
and tricked its tunnel
with her green green fingernails.
Gim says he's always loved her but Phantom Girl,
that blabbermouth,
wants to know why he would take her somewhere as tacky
as the Alps
for their honeymoon. Meanwhile, Star Boy is wearing this new outfit,
a starfield?
His costume, it's made of stars.

Wildfire Loves Dawnstar

When time comes for new applicants,
you would rather whistle for Lamprey or Nightwind—
but of course you would, Wildfire, your weakness
for Legion trainees well-known, wonder
for Lamprey's light and her hair like kelp,
wonder for Nightwind, her cloak's active static.
Who do they remind you of but Dawnstar,
she whose wings widen to accommodate worlds?
Dawnstar, from whose essence emanates the ultimate
echolocation. There is nothing she cannot find
or follow save your human form, consumed in fire.
You, now, poured into a suit, selfless without surface,
mancoat hung by tatter on a wire, wire
your very public secret. False foot in rocket boot,
false hand in rocket gauntlet. Graced with wire
and glass, smoked black where once the face was.
What does her face reflected in that glass remind
you of but the radiation red of your palm's print
wherever your prototype flesh brushed and burned the girl?
Wildfire. No body owned, so no one. Bluster
instead of human pause, antienergy, antic, you
are *not*, Drake Burroughs, and she *is*, so enfleshed
her naked name speaks all her singular selves.
Dawnstar, pride and protégé, your never-wife,
now teacher, once taught. She wishes there was a you
inside this fabric to kiss
but you both know that there is not.

Shadow Lass Loves Mon-El

exit invocations of the Phantom Zone

what speaks speaks to echo

beautiful Daxamite drunk on lead, its dullness deadly

propelled to phantom beautiful ghost

in his absent arms we age to forty then four hundred

continents trim and ripple

beautiful drunk with his polarized perspective

truly tomorrowed in his saintly blood suit

because all speech is echo when he said love

his name

first said as forgotten that it was unsaid

as his name said love

make Mon-El's flesh apparent under our hands

his blush backward his pulse finally a presence

his immortal cheek now fire red now flesh now wine red

he's here his blush beautiful already unfading

Elemental

The lad values gold less than lead, the lad denies élan vital.
The last living member of the most envied race
knows that life arises from accident,
from a force with no more meaning than impact mechanics,
he knows that matter doesn't matter.
All that matter is derives from smash, snap, and decay,
one atom's worth of shifting numbers.
Addition and subtraction are both transformation.
Mostly hydrogen, sometimes carbon. Mostly nitrogen, sometimes oxygen.
When he concentrates, an alloy appears,
but it doesn't appear from nowhere.
When he shakes the chain he compounds the problem.
Sometimes noble, sometimes inert,
but more than half of everything is nothing.
Sometimes sulfur, mostly phosphorous.
The remainder is lack. The remainder is dark.

Brainiac 5 Generates Autocritique

Every case I make is oblique. Dative, I take it.
I do not get to the point; I do not see what it's for.

Datapoints are of three kinds: binary or yes/no,
vector or array, and integer, which must perforce be real.

Endless binaries branch into de facto chaos. I take
wrong turns. But vector's even more hectic. With ballistics

I plot where you will be on the basis of where you were,
yet because you remain in motion, my equations never catch up.

Integers, however: these are real when they are rational,
real when they are irrational. I wish I couldn't say the same.

Reckless, ragged, I throw myself against unrealizable goals
with *I think I can* and *I think I can* and *I think, I can.*

Presence of clinical distance doesn't mean absence
of clinical interest. Sometimes I go insane, and when I go,

I sound just like I do before I left. But I don't know
any other way to talk about it. I never met a problem

I didn't think I could solve, which is the eruption of rationality
into unreason. I thought I could save you from death

even though you were dead before I was born. I found you,
even though you were never lost. How close could we ever get?

Am I cold? Am I getting warmer? The closer you approach
the farther you recede. This was always the way it would be.

That didn't stop me. Rational, unreasonable. I did this for you,
I did this to myself. I went looking for you, I took you to heart.

I do not understand what you do not understand is the perfect sentence
even though the perfect sentence is also the perfect sentence.

The weight and motion of a thousand years must create detrition.
That is why my manner is so flat. My mind, worn smooth by friction.

Instructions for the Use of Telepathic Plug

If basalt-headed gods of apocalypse switch civilizations and the planets with them, then six billion become ensorcelled with might. If they fly diplomatic planetoids apart with their en masse migrations.

step swift into your transsuit

The Focal Example of Invisible Kids

seen not believed

let us recollect and resurrect Lyle

lick every lie from his lips and taste

then unseen and just so

let us savor his serum

the solution for sight

his girl suspended between dimensions

but "see" is insufficient

in a transparent palm

never heard and never seen

"see" through the water cupped

or through the sea's strata

to fall asleep was Lyle's second-best trick

when he closed his eyes

we eulogize him the second smartest

the first was to die

everyone else disappeared

the best Earth had to offer

but the second invisible kid shares

that the mess of the world maintains

invisibility acts on reason not sense

with his predecessor an error

when we erase our gaze

faith not the vanished body

Lyle's lies were invisible stories

the essential invisible

a picture a portrait

as is proof of love

justice as well as judgment

time-lapse elapsed

in home movies of the original invisible kid

action rattles the screen

events like sheets of glass

to recollect is to gather again

the memory of drink dear and inadequate

serum seen in the glass shines

a concoction of perfect clarity

detail is lost to deterioration

in invisible hands

absent memories remain

blind

once there was a boy

motes of dust glint gone

much unclear occurs

set one atop the next

what you cannot believe

as holographs of dead lovers

printless without character

dumb to itself

opaque snow falls to water

their motion unnoted

where are you, Invisible Kid?

we ask the obvious

then there was not

then there was

Instructions for the Use of Telepathic Plug

If the Legion of Super-Villains, awful analogues, finally come courting. If grandiloquent Lightning Lord, then crafty Cosmic King. If ridiculously lethal Radiation Roy, then imperious, one-fisted Tyr. If annihilating Neutrax, then Terrus, clever coward. If murderously single-minded Nemesis Kid, then just half-bad Spider Girl. If methodical Magno Lad, then the wide-eyed folly of the Silver Slasher. If vain, gay-hearted Lazon, then must the malignant Mist Master. If that ill-tempered zealot Ol-Vir, then creepy Chameleon Chief. If paper-thin Ron-Karr, then scowling Titania, bellicose bruiser. If hatefully principled Hunter, then self-righteous Micro Lad. If irritable Esper Lass, then effortlessly alien Zymyr. If Sun Emperor, true sadist, visits old Orando in summertime and kisses a kitchen maid to char.

in case of emergency, shatter the glass

Dream Girl Only Dreams of Darkness

The origin of vanity
is a bad night's sleep.
Down Dreamy goes,
a blue caul descends
over her baby face,
her unconscious staggers and gasps.
She goes to sleep and wakes up,
she goes to sleep to wake up,
she is never more asleep
than when she is awake.
She sees one catastrophe after another,
nacreous, nauseous, seductive.
In dreaming she extracts an absolute
from what the woken only know by half.
Her work is to winnow the real.
If her prophecies always come true,
and they do,
our work is to prove her fooled by truth.
We know what you saw, we'll say,
but you must have misread the text.
We make of wakefulness a stage.
We act whatever play she dreams next.

The Death of Karate Kid

he had thought he faced it before
but either he did not or he did and turned away
but regardless he always said he wanted
to go out fighting

the way he came in and the way
he built his days
just as he built his skills
and became so masterful he grew super

but to wish to go out fighting
is different when you are being beaten to death
by the one foe you know you cannot defeat
and so he cannot be blamed for a moment's cowardice

though he should be praised for bravery
even if that too lasts for only a moment
he still wanted to die a hero's death
the wish of every responsible teen

that is also a fear that he wouldn't die
or at least not in time
but this time he did and brutally
a sacrifice with horrific scars

the sun sets on this backward planet
and the queen who gained a throne
but lost her consort burns the bower
and his body burning still bears its chains

What to Expect: Crime and Punishment

What do you do with something like Klim the synthetic criminal with his zutronic brain?

At one extreme, consider the planet Lythyl, where thanks to the Freedom of Behavior Act what constitutes crime has been negotiated into nothingness.

At Glacier Point they queue up for yet another round of psychic rehabilitation.

The law will develop ever less subjective instruments: *Science* Police.

For instance, ponder the Interrogator, the probes of which finesse and detect one's innermost thoughts. *You cannot deceive me*, it states, *my truth-value indicator prohibits it.*

On Takron-Galtos, the prison planet, the Science Police, too, have a rehabilitation room, an encephalodetector.

Yet the Science Police once again request assistance on Takron-Galtos.

Every time a certain subset of villains break free, they do worse than their worst.

From the shallowest motives thus come the bloodiest murders.

Eventually we will come to perfectly interpret risk.

We will never disinter recidivists.

On Labyrinth we will bury them.

Possibility Trumps Brainiac 5

They say God always provides. Who are *they?* What is *God?*
There once was an adventure of the Legion of Super-Infants.

I won't tell the tale, which sounds tall, though it's true.
It was temporal, whimsical. Of all aesthetics I hate whimsicality

the most. A true story can be silly in the telling, true,
but I worry more over the story, the truth of which is silliness.

I hate magic and God is a magical being, if God is at all,
which God is not, for only that which can be, is. God is love,

God is truth, God is beauty, beauty is truth, I love the truth,
I am confused. I can explain why I find beauty, but not where.

"All kinds of energy exist" and "somewhere beyond our universe"
are phrases I hate. Existence, uh, includes all of everything;

somewhere excludes anywhere beyond everywhere. The universe
has limits. It cannot have limits. Don't tell me how wonderful!—

it's terrible in that it creates fear, it's horrible because
it horrifies me. I prefer the subluminal to the sublime.

I would take forever to go nowhere rather than go somewhere
by means of magic. I hate magic, except when it's a trick,

when it isn't magical, when an antiquarian vaudevillian yanks
a silk flower out of a silk sleeve and fakes a sneeze. I thank

God to spite God, that of which I cannot speak, for one cannot
speak of that which is not. I cite an idea of God, which refers

to nothing, which is. If it isn't magic it looks like magic,
the flower you must know to know the magician's flower is not.

Do you know where flowers come from? From flowers, enfleurage.
God provides, God denies, voila. Magic. The flower of carnage.

There's a point at which supernal ceases to mean excellent and starts to mean impossible. Ceases to be science, in other words, and becomes superstition. If supernormal is, then supernatural cannot be. Superrealism cannot become superphysical. I'm trying to make sense of this, because I'm surrounded by teenagers who don't make any sense, which is something I know how to make. You would think supersensible would mean sensibility above. But it means beyond, which is the reverse. And that's perverse.

Yours,
Brainiac 5

Snow Falls on Alternate Metropolis

Unscheduled snow, actual snow,
the random weather that proves
the inversion of the magic/science ratio.
In alternative Metropolis,
minor characters are major threats,
crude brutes have grown fey,
the dead live again.
Ferro Lad would be returned to us,
but we aren't ourselves; we're them,
and where we are celebrated
they are hounded underground.
For us he wore a mask of chrome,
but for them he dresses in rustic leather.
Magic is more cruel than science, it seems,
for it has driven even good witches
to church and made men theologize
what we knew as a matter of proof.
Because he knows things shouldn't be this way
the boy who would have been Ferro Lad
helps cast a spell, ice reddened
with blood sigils. He upturns the hourglass.
The last thing he sees—ghostly, unfamiliar—us.
Constellations pulls themselves undone,
and then the boy and the snow are gone.

Brainiac 5 Cracks His Head
against the Iron Curtain of Time

What do you get for the girl who is everything?
Once we believed the future could be good, because

once we believed the future could be. It couldn't,
it could only be. We have no future together.

No utopia is eternal. Endlessness pretends to heaven,
which brought to earth requires transcendent death,

the very state I wanted to be greater than, to surpass.
Disaggregate with me, break this sad fact constituent.

I can never know on which side of dreaming I wax hypnagogic.
Do I wake or do I sleep? I worked so hard to be half in love.

Like all ages and eras, you had a set span. I broke the universe
to cross it. All the troubles, all the troubled, but you first.

Stay in twilight, Supergirl, and I will pretend your sun
is ever on the edge of dawn. Wake me, tell me it's time

to go. It is time. It was time. I knew. I know.

The Persistence of Espionage

Chameleon Boy rides the maglev to Montauk,
nobody on that train, its bare tremble
socialist, synthetic slide down the future,
its dead white world's fair.
Empty stations, empty agents—
no more buttons, no more coats.
Reep Daggle dreams of Durla, her imagine ocean,
her drowned city neither coral nor spire.
Its epics are a collective colossus,
generations beached and bleached,
over two hundred tons of elegant elbow
sunk in diatomaceous sand, fallen body
of friend and foe and family,
right angle of the wrist risen to vertigo.
In the last exploit of the Espionage Squad,
all the useless heroes will die
except Chameleon Boy, his neural net
polyform and plasticene, eternal.
But yes, Phantom Girl, Shrinking Violet,
Invisible Kid. A lost city looms
behind the wrecked and ruined dunes.
Forty thousand colors, eighty thousand ages.
The world is not like this at all.